Discove

of Bitcoin

A Full Guide to Understand
the Biggest Cryptocurrency
Today and Get Started with It

By

Joe Bears

The information provided herein is stated to be truthful and consistent, in that any liability, in terms of inattention or otherwise, by any usage or abuse of any policies, processes, or directions contained within is the solitary and utter responsibility of the recipient reader. Under no circumstances will any legal responsibility or blame be held against the publisher for any reparation, damages, or monetary loss due to the information herein, either directly or indirectly.

Respective authors own all copyrights not held by the publisher.

The information herein is offered for informational purposes solely and is universal as so. The presentation of the information is without a contract or any type of guarantee assurance.

The trademarks that are used are without any consent, and the publication of the trademark is without permission or backing by the trademark owner. All trademarks and brands within this book are for clarifying purposes only and are owned by the owners themselves, not affiliated with this document.

Table of Contents

Introduction

Bitcoin is a virtual currency or a means of electronic exchange used to acquire products and services like any other currency. But this currency is decentralized, meaning that there is no authority or control entity responsible for its issuance and registration of its movements. It consists of a cryptographic key that is associated with a virtual wallet that withdraws and receives payments.

In order to make an exchange, each user must have a cryptographic key, and the system allows for discounting the amount of bitcoin to the buyer and increases the amount of bitcoin in the account of the seller.

There is no middleman when making a withdrawal or payment. You can have several accounts, and the system operates 24 hours a day.

It should be noted that the bitcoin and the key associated with the cryptographic code must be verified for its execution.

Chapter 1: The Basics and History of Bitcoin

It is the first known digital currency that is running on a technology called a blockchain. It is entirely decentralized. Therefore, no one has control over it. It also is known as electronic money or digital currency. However, it is a peer-peer payment system. Therefore, it's software. It has no real presence whatsoever, as it's growing on your computer's hard drive. In fact, on every computer that exists in the world.

This currency will never be touched by anyone as it only exists in a digital form. With regards to its value, it does seem to fluctuate. However, it has kept itself steady for a long period: moreover, continuously increasing. Back in 2008, it began to compete with the dollar—when one Bitcoin was equal to $0.05. However, in June 2017, one Bitcoin has reached $2,912.00, its highest value as of yet. Over the years, Bitcoin not only proved that it could reach its highest over and over again, but it has increased its value higher than what we have ever experienced with any other currency on Mother Earth.

As of June 2017, looking at the currency exchange, Bitcoin against the dollar for the last ten years, I can tell that it will keep on growing.

My personal opinion is that we will keep on seeing Bitcoins increase in value, especially around each four-year mark. Why would I say that? Well, let's just say that I have my reasons.

How Many Bitcoins Are Out There?

Good question, and you can calculate it yourself. Of course, it all depends on the date and time you're reading this book.

So, let's look at some of the facts that we know for sure before beginning any complex calculations. The first 50 Bitcoins were created on the 31st of October 2008. Then, 50 more Bitcoins were created every 10 minutes until 2012. After 2012, the amount of Bitcoin production reduced to half—meaning every 10 minutes, 25 new Bitcoins were created until 2016.

Since 2016, the process has followed the same principles—meaning, every 10 minutes, 12.5 Bitcoins will be created until 2020. This process will keep on going until 2140 until there will be 21 million Bitcoins on the market.

Bad Reputation

In case you haven't heard of the Dark Web, let me explain a little about it. I could dedicate a whole book to the Dark Web, and I might do it in the future. I am not interested in trading drugs or guns online. However, just because that is a list of things that can be purchased on the Dark Web does not mean I will ever be participating in those markets.

What you must understand is that the Internet as we know it—through search engines like google, yahoo, or Bing—isn't the only web out there. There is another, and It's known as the darknet; it can be reached through another search engine called TOR. TOR network is also known as an onion router or onion network. TOR is capable of hiding the IP Address of the end-user; therefore, making whatever is done on the Internet completely untraceable.

Even your internet service provider wouldn't know what website you visited, except that you have visited the TOR network. You might look around and see for yourself what kind of services are offered there, but it's up to you. I have visited the Dark Web before to get a feel for it, and the more you look around, the more you will find ugly services. And I am sorry to mention this, but the things I have seen are disgusting, and for those who can be easily upset, I would not recommend it at all. My point is that the guns and drug traders on TOR ask for payment in the form of Bitcoin. Bitcoin is untraceable, as well as the TOR network. Therefore, the Dark Web is a haven for criminals.

Do criminals use Bitcoin too? They sure do. In fact, they have no other choice when it comes to illegal goods or services online. Before you close this book and walk away from the idea of using Bitcoin because criminals are using it too, please think twice. Bitcoin wasn't created for criminals. Bitcoin was designed for everyone and please don't forget about those 3 billion people that Bitcoin can save when it comes to financing.

Another issue that happens over and over is that Bitcoin accounts get hacked, and people are left with empty wallets. Please don't misunderstand this point. It's not the Bitcoin that is hacked, but the end-user level victim's Computers or mobile devices. The value of Bitcoin has become enormous, and hackers do educate themselves too. Therefore, they have changed their game once again and realized that hacking Bitcoin accounts is profitable and untraceable; so, why not do it—especially do it on a grand scale? This issue has been addressed, and if you decide to own a wallet, you must make sure that you always back up your wallet, as well, always have all the security features enabled. Some of these security features are like 2-step authentications that don't require much learning or time; still, better to be secured than assuming that hackers will never find you.

So, because many people have fallen victim to Bitcoin account hacks, they have stopped trading or investing in Bitcoin or any digital cryptocurrency.

Wikileaks

You might be familiar with the website WikiLeaks—a non-profit organization responsible for publishing secrets and classified information anonymously. Of course, individual governments are not happy with the website, and they have issued the site to be shut down. The site requires basic maintenance, as well as security, and the only contributors able to help have had to use Bitcoin. As a result, the website has stayed alive to this day. This is one of the most famous examples. However, there are countless causes that people have been able to provide help to others, even to the other side of the planet, using Bitcoin.

A Rumor about a Decrease in Value

The most common speculations and accusations against Bitcoin are its possible fluctuation. Why is that? Well, people often say, "What if there is another type of cryptocurrency that could compete with Bitcoin using the same underlying technology, the Blockchain? Would Bitcoin lose its value?" The accusations are indeed possible, but looking at the history of Bitcoin value, only significant increases happened, even with 734 other cryptocurrencies. I am not a futurist, but after analyzing the facts, I think it's fair to say that Bitcoin is on the rise and will not stop for a long time.

What Can You Buy?

Well, you can buy anything on the Dark Web—of course—I do not recommend that, as you might come across criminals who would try to steal or hack into your Bitcoin wallet. Some cybercriminals would even try to blackmail you. However, if you do not provide your details, you should be just fine. Realistically, more services are excepting Bitcoin, such as Hotels, Restaurants, Coffee shops, even some takeaway shops are now offering payment methods using Bitcoin.

Large retail companies are also accepting Bitcoin, such as Shopify, TigerDirect, and many more. To see how wide range it can be already, you have to look around where you live. The big cities have all sort of offerings, such as:

- Theatre

- Taxi Service
- Bicycle rent
- Private Jets
- Pubs

Also, you may consider other large companies that are now accepting Bitcoin, such as:

- Dell
- Microsoft
- Zynga
- Reddit
- Wordpress.com
- Subway
- Expedia.com
- Virgin Galactic
- OK Cupid
- Stream

- Alza
- Lionsgate Films
- Badoo... and many more

By using Gift cards, multiple applications also allow customers to purchase on websites, such as:

- Amazon.com
- Walmart
- Target
- Nike
- GAP
- BEBE
- Sears
- Papa Johns
- Best Buy
- iTunes

- eBay
- Starbucks
- Zappos
- CVS Pharmacy
- The HOME depot... and much more.

I wanted you to see that some of the largest companies are already adapting to the idea of accepting Bitcoin. Moreover, to understand the range of goods and services that can be purchased, please see the list of categories that you may choose from:

- Airline
- Automotive
- Beauty
- Clothing
- Department Stores
- e-Commerce

- Electronics
- Gas
- Gifts and Toys
- Grocery
- Health
- Home and Garden
- Home improvement
- Hotel
- Jewellery
- Movies
- Pets
- Restaurants
- Shoes
- Sporting goods

As you see, the categories keep on growing, and if you are more interested in what stores you can pay using Bitcoin, you might check what you have nearby you or what online platforms can deliver to your area.

Why Is Not Everyone Using Bitcoin?

Well, the reality is that most people who are already aware of the existence of Bitcoin are too lazy to do some research for a better understanding of the potentials.

Personally, I first heard about Bitcoin in 2013, and I didn't look at it that much. What I understood was that Bitcoin was some form of online payment method, and most criminals were using it because it's untraceable. That's it. I keep up with the news, and somehow, no one seems to talk about it unless there is a significant Cyberattack, and the hackers would demand ransom, or some payment, in the form of Bitcoin.

Anyhow, at the end of 2015, I heard about Bitcoin again when I was studying Network Security, so I mentioned it to my friend Rob. He said that, yes; he was aware of Bitcoin, and its worth was like $300. When Rob said it, I couldn't believe that one Bitcoin was worth $300! Of course, I still didn't understand what Bitcoin was. I thought that it was like a real physical coin; I still had no clue that it only exists in a digital form. Then another friend Viktor, who overheard what we were talking about, said that he couldn't believe that I had never heard of Bitcoin before! So, I said, "Yes, I did hear about it, but I didn't know that it's worth so much." I started thinking more and more about it, and I began to do some research. A little later, I had an idea to make Bitcoin using my old laptop! So, I told Viktor and Rob that I heard that computers could generate Bitcoin, and if it's worth like $300 each, I might be able to produce one or two every week. Obviously, I had no clue what I was talking about, and they told me off that it's not that easy. However, they couldn't explain to me how it's exactly done. They said that I was thinking like a hacker, and I shouldn't be like that, as it's for criminals. But I stated that it sounds like an exciting technology. They replied, "OK, so why do you need Bitcoin? What do you want to buy? Do you want to buy something on the Dark Web?" They made me speechless, so I didn't say anything anymore. However, I secretly begin to learn as much as possible about Bitcoin, and of course, that leads me to another interesting technology called Blockchain.

My point is that most people have been misled by fake news, and for those that might be interested, it takes a long time to understand how Bitcoin or Blockchain works. Therefore, most people give up research and will not get involved in any way.

Chapter 2: How Does Bitcoin Work?

At this point, you might be interested in learning how you can obtain Bitcoin. But before you skip to that part, it would be valuable to understand the inner workings of this new technology. It isn't a necessity to know how Bitcoin works in order to use it—so you can skip ahead if you like—but I do recommend that users familiarize themselves with the basics, so they aren't completely in the dark when it comes to their own money.

Public-Key Cryptography

To understand Bitcoin, you need to understand the principle of public-key cryptography. While the details are complicated, it essentially means that each user that wishes to communicate with another user has two keys (groups of numbers). One key is public; everyone can see this series of numbers. The other is private; only the individual user has this key.

Here's an example of how public-key cryptography is used. To send a secret letter, Alice would encrypt the letter using Betty's public key. Alice then sends this letter along. Betty receives the letter and then decrypts it using her private key.

The reason public-key cryptography is powerful is that it doesn't matter if someone else—let's say, Charlie—intercepts the letter. Without the private key that only Betty has, he can't decrypt it. This technology allows everyone to see the encrypted letter, but only the intended recipient can actually read it.

Millions of Deposit Boxes

How does Bitcoin use public-key cryptography? Earlier I mentioned the Blockchain—a public record of all Bitcoin transactions. Think of the Blockchain as having millions of safety deposit boxes made out of bulletproof glass. The boxes have varying amounts of Bitcoin inside them but are securely locked. Even though everyone can see what each box contains, only the owners can unlock them.

These deposit boxes are called *public keys*—*everyone* can see the numbers (also called an address) and the amount within the boxes. The owners of each deposit box access their Bitcoin using their *private key*. While everyone can see the deposit boxes and the amount of Bitcoin inside, only the owners of the private key can use the money.

In our earlier example, Alice sent Betty a message that only Betty could read. Bitcoin works the same way, except we aren't sending letters but instead information telling your deposit box to give some of your Bitcoin to another deposit box. To use the example again, here's how it works. Alice wants to send 1 BTC to Betty, so she sends out a message to the entire network. This message includes Betty's public address (the location of her deposit box), the amount of Bitcoin she wants to send to

Betty, and a digital signature that verifies she is the owner of the private key to her own deposit box.

When Alice sends this message to the network, other network users verify that this message is accurate. If all the numbers match up, then the transaction gets put into a block (a collection of other transactions), and this block eventually gets published in the Blockchain. Once that occurs, the rest of the network recognizes that Alice's deposit box is 1.0 BTC smaller than before, and Betty's deposit box has grown by 1.0 BTC. Since the Blockchain is a public ledger that extends all the way back to the first Bitcoin transaction, it knows the exact amount of Bitcoin in every deposit box that exists.

Mining for Coins

Now you understand how transactions take place, but you might be wondering where Bitcoins even come from in the first place. Remember how I mentioned some network users verify the transactions are accurate and then include them in a block to be published to the entire network? This process requires significant computing power, so why would other users be willing to do this? Because they are rewarded with Bitcoin!

Devoting your computer to processing transactions is called mining. Miners verify transactions, and as they are doing so, they are looking for the solution to a mathematical problem. If they are the first to find the answer, the code allows them to publish the block of transactions to the rest of the network. Whoever publishes the block gets a reward, currently set at 25 BTC. This reward halves every few years so that the amount of Bitcoin never grows too quickly. Also, as more people devote more computing power to the network in order to increase the chance of getting a block reward, the difficulty of mining increases. The code automatically adjusts the difficulty of the mathematical problem so that a new block is mined approximately every 10 minutes.

A Chain of Blocks

One more important thing to mention about the blocks—they are built on each other in a chain (hence the term blockchain). It is imperative to have a continuous and chronological record of all transactions; this ensures the amounts of each and every deposit box have been accounted for. In order to do this, each block has two additional elements apart from the transactions. One is a much-shortened snapshot of all previous blocks, called a hash. This hash ensures that the Blockchain is building on the previous blocks, all the way back to the original block (called the genesis block). The second aspect is the answer to the complicated math problem the miners need to solve. The next block cannot be mined until the problem has been solved, ensuring that blocks are created in chronological order. As of June 2013, there have been more than 238,000 blocks published in the Blockchain.

In this way, the Bitcoin ecosystem keeps evolving. Transactions get compiled into new blocks, the blocks are published to the rest of the network in a continuous chain, miners get rewards for their work, and those new Bitcoins are used for transactions, starting the cycle over again.

Network Verification

How is this system kept in check? After all, Alice could send a message saying that she has 5.0 BTC to send to Betty, even though her deposit box only has 2.0 BTC. There are many ways that dishonest users could attempt to trick the system, but fortunately, it's virtually impossible. This is because Bitcoin is a decentralized system where all transactions are public and require verification from the rest of the network. If Alice tried to send more coins than she had, the recipient would immediately check the balance of the account, recognize this, and reject the transaction. It would never make its way into the block, and the rest of the network would never even see the false transaction. This verification is done in the code of the Bitcoin program itself, so it is nearly instant.

How to Obtain Bitcoin?

So, you're sold on the benefits of having Bitcoin. Great! But how can you get them? There are a variety of methods, some simpler than others, but I'll walk through each of them for you.

Before I talk about how to get coins, here is a warning: it is important to know how to properly store and secure them. Your coins are only as safe as you make them. I'll discuss the different ways to safely handle your Bitcoins in the next section, so make sure you've read that section before going out and buying any.

There are four ways to obtain Bitcoin: receiving them for free, selling your goods and services for them, buying them directly, or mining them.

Digital Faucet: Free Coins?

Yes, you can get free Bitcoins. There are multiple websites that give free coins to get users started (called faucets). However, with the rise in Bitcoin's value, many faucets have shut down, and the remaining ones give out minuscule amounts of coins. While they were valuable when Bitcoin was in its infancy, I wouldn't bother spending time with faucets today.

Sell Your Stuff

You can sell your goods or services to obtain Bitcoin. Some eBay-like websites only deal in Bitcoin, such as Betemit. A quick search on Craigslist for the term "Bitcoin" will show many dealers offering the products for a coin. Internet forums exist for Bitcoin users to buy and sell their own merchandise, such as Reddit's Bit market. This is a relatively simple way to obtain Bitcoin if you have anything valuable you don't mind parting with.

While most items offered for sale by Bitcoin users aren't very expensive, there are some examples of very large transactions. A Texas family sold their Porsche for 300 BTC recently. A Canadian man put his house on the market for Bitcoin.

Purchasing Bitcoins

The most common way to obtain Bitcoin is by purchasing them. There are many different avenues to purchase Bitcoin, but two ways are the most common.

One is to purchase Bitcoins locally and in person. This frequently occurs if you know someone with Bitcoin. Avid Bitcoin users are often happy to sell a small amount to other users in order to get them started.

However, you certainly don't need to know a guy in order to buy them locally. A popular website called "LocalBitcoins" allows you to search for sellers in your area and then arrange a meeting to make the transaction. These personal transactions do carry some amount of risk since you have no guarantee they will send you the coin once you hand over the money (or vice versa!). However, the website uses a reputational system so that each seller has reviews from previous buyers. In this way, it is in a seller's interest to ensure they don't cheat their clients. The vast majority of users report positive interactions with LocalBitcoins.

The second way to obtain Bitcoin is probably the most common of all: purchase them from an exchange or affiliated payment processor. Exchanges are businesses that will buy and sell Bitcoin for various national currencies, such as dollars, pounds, euro, or yen.

Exchanges have been a critical part of Bitcoin's expansion. Originally, miners were the primary users of Bitcoin since there wasn't really a marketplace to sell their coins. Once exchanges became popular, coins could be purchased by anyone, no need to have a computer set up to mine coins.

There are many exchanges available. Some of them are primarily useful because they serve a specific region or deal primarily in a certain currency. Here is a list of the most popular ones.

- **Mt. Gox.** This is, by far, the largest exchange for Bitcoin. Mt. Gox was an early entry into the market, and for some time, they had nearly 100% market share as a Bitcoin exchange. This has slowly declined over time and is now somewhere near 60%. Mt. Gox is based in Japan but transacts in dollars, pounds, euros, and yen. They have drawn much criticism from the community for not acting in a professional or timely manner and causing some turmoil in the Bitcoin markets, but they are still the industry leader by a long shot.

- **CampBX.** This exchange is based in the US and deals in dollars. While Mt. Gox no longer accepts payments through online payment processor Dwolla, CampBX still does.
- **BitStamp.** An exchange located in Europe, dealing with multiple currencies.
- BTC-E. A Russian exchange, dealing in multiple currencies and also dealing in cryptocurrencies other than Bitcoin.

- **Coinbase.** This service, established in 2012, operates out of California. It allows you to link your bank account directly to their service, enabling users to buy Bitcoin instantly from their bank account. There is a limit on how many Bitcoin you can buy or sell with their service.
- **BitInstant.** A service similar to Coinbase, except you don't need a bank account. For a fee, you can deposit cash at local stores in the US such as CVS or Walmart and using a payment processor, and you'll receive some Bitcoin minutes later.

This is only a handful of the services out there you can use to obtain Bitcoin.

Despite there being many ways to obtain Bitcoin, it often takes patience to finally have some coin in your wallet. Most of the exchanges require identification in order for them to comply with their nation's laws. The process of verifying identification can take days or even weeks. Mt. Gox is famous for having a queue of people waiting for identification that has stretched into the thousands!

Once you're verified, you then need to fund the exchange. For some time, one of the most popular ways to fund Mt. Gox accounts was Dwolla, an inexpensive online payment processor. However, in May 2013, the US government shut down Mt. Gox's account that used Dwolla, citing incorrect permitting. Now getting funds to the largest exchange requires a wire transfer or using another payment processor.

Dwolla can still be used at CampBX and a few other places, but it's unclear for how long Dwolla will still be a viable exchange funding method. Given the uncertainty around Dwolla for now, what is the best way to obtain coins?

This depends on your level of patience, acceptance of fees, and desired anonymity. If you are patient, want low fees, and don't mind your coins tied to your identity, I would suggest using Coinbase. It is simple to set up; you just register an account with an e-mail address and then link a bank account. You can choose to instantly link the account using your online banking login credentials. As trustworthy as Coinbase is, I would recommend their second option. They make two small deposits into your account, and you verify your account based on entering the correct amount deposited. This process does take several days from start to finish, but there are few fees.

If you are impatient and need Bitcoin today, and you can tolerate higher fees, I would suggest using BitInstant. It lives up to its name—once you fill out a form on their site, you go to a local store that offers money transfer services (there are many), deposit the exact amount requested, and only minutes later, the coins are deposited in your wallet. Because you need to fill out your personal information, this method also isn't anonymous.

If you want anonymity, use LocalBitcoin and transact for cash in person. Obviously, be careful doing this. As I mentioned earlier, most users report positive results, but there are some scammers in the Bitcoin community who may literally take your money and run. Look for sellers who have a good reputation online.

Be very wary of individuals selling Bitcoin outside of reputable communities. If anyone wants to use PayPal, especially to buy your Bitcoins, that is a warning sign. PayPal isn't a good idea to buy or sell Bitcoin because transactions are reversible, meaning someone could receive the coins then take back their payment.

Do some quick Google searches of the exchanges and services I suggested, and find out which works best for you. But remember, don't buy until you've read the section on securing your coins.

Mining for Bitcoin

There is one last way to obtain Bitcoin, and that is to mine them. For most readers, I doubt this is a viable option, so you can read this section if you have an interest in learning about mining, but feel free to skip ahead.

As I mentioned earlier, mining Bitcoin means that you are lending your computer power to verify other user's transactions while searching for the solution to the mathematical problem. The miner that finds this solution first will publish the next block and receive a 25 BTC reward.

25 BTC created approximately every 10 minutes is a lot of money, so it's easy to understand why many people want to be Bitcoin miners.

Here's the bad news: The train has already left the station when it comes to Bitcoin mining. It's very unlikely that anyone who would start today and invest the significant resources of time, computing power, electricity, and money into running a mining rig will recoup that cost for a very, very long time—if ever.

If that's true, then why are there so many miners out there? Because mining used to be very profitable. Previously, miners used the CPUs to run the program that mined coins. After a while, someone realized that using a GPU (the graphics card) would actually solve the mathematical solution much more quickly. More people began running GPU rigs with multiple video cards. As more people entered the mining market, the chances of anyone getting the block reward dwindled.

Miners worked around this problem by joining mining pools. They contributed their computer power to the pool of miners, and in return, if the next block was found by the pool, they divided the block reward amongst everyone participating. This worked well for a while, although mining pools dealt with new problems such as storage space and cooling their rigs down.

Then a new development in mining came along: Application Specific Integrated Circuits or ASICs. These rigs were specifically designed to mine Bitcoin—and that is all they can do! Because they do nothing but mine Bitcoin, they don't require nearly as much energy as a standard mining rig. A rig that uses little power and is orders of magnitude better than the previous technology was a significant step forward for miners, but it came with a price. These new machines are in high demand, and so they are expensive—very expensive. Finding a quality, ASIC could easily cost thousands of dollars.

This creates a dilemma for anyone looking to enter into the mining market because now there are so many other players and such advanced technology that the chances of you actually getting a block reward are very small unless you make a significant investment (both upfront and continuing). You would be far better off taking those thousands of dollars and simply buying the Bitcoin directly!

I don't recommend readers attempt to mine Bitcoin. That is becoming a specialized service taken on by increasing larger players with access to infrastructure. Gone are the days where running the Bitcoin client on your laptop computer could easily bring in hundreds of Bitcoins.

Chapter 3: Fundamentals of Bitcoin Mining

As with every existing technology, when it comes to Blockchain, it is also true that there are only a select few individuals who are interested in how things work. Therefore, I would like to congratulate you on deciding to take your interest to the next level. Most people are only interested in listening to music; they never learn how the CD player works. Of course, there are new ways of listening to music or audiobooks. Still, this is one of the all-time favorite examples that I have always used throughout the years when I'm just about to explain something to someone who isn't interested in what I am about to say.

The reality is that you don't have to understand how the CD Player works, neither how the music is transferred wirelessly, using Bluetooth technology, to the speakers that provide you with your favorite tunes. This is fine; however, each time you learn a new word, you are creating an additional brain cell, leading to you increasing your IQ, and in turn, you become more intelligent. Furthermore, you will decrease your chances of losing all your brain cells. It has been researched that once an average human being turns 30–40 years old, brain cells begin to die, literally keep disappearing, and it is not much you can do about it. Each decade an average human loses between 5–10% of his brain capacity; of course, it depends on many circumstances. But the overall average is 7%. Brain cells will die—no matter what. However, what you can do is to keep on creating additional brain cells by learning new words and new skills, really anything that is new to your brain. It has also been researched that learning a new language can help you grow your IQ, creating a tremendous amount of new brain cells.

Which new language? You might begin to learn German, Italian, or French. However, when it comes to technology, there are other languages too: C+, C++, Python, SQL, JAVA, Pascal, PHP, and hundreds more that you can grasp. Each minute of your interest and learning will divide you from the crowd.

This book will focus on the technology called Blockchain. Although it is relatively new, once you take a closer look at it, you will understand that the underlying technologies that allow the

Blockchain to run have existed previously. I will reveal each of these technologies in great detail as well; due to Blockchain's innovations, there are some new protocols that must be addressed in the following chapters.

If you have not read my first book, Blockchain for beginners—Volume 1, I would highly recommend starting with that first, so this book will not be that hard to understand. Nevertheless, I will provide a little overview of what the Blockchain is in few sentences.

The most important point to note is that Bitcoin and Blockchain are not the same things. A blockchain is a system that has its first implementation on the Bitcoin network. Bitcoin is a kind of Blockchain. Bitcoin, on the other hand, is just a cryptocurrency available to replace fiat currencies. Nonetheless, several citizens would be turned off by the concept at first.

Blockchain has solved the problem that we have always faced, and that is trust. Using blockchain technology enables us to avoid trusted third-party services. Therefore, any payment or exchange over the Internet will be between 2 parties only. This is revolutionary, as we can expand the trust gap, and the market of the future will not only be faster and cheaper but will have no limitations, such as age, race, sex, occupation, nationality, or anything like that.

Blockchain uses a distributed ledger system to keep all records that have ever been registered on the Blockchain. The records are trusted by proof-of-work.

Miners have an important role as well, and the two most significant topics they must address are:

1. Trying to validate transactions on a continuous basis.

2. Adding additional value to a device that already exists.

Individuals or any Bitcoin citizen could be miner, but, with time, several big corporations have emerged, such as Genesis Mining, where you can enter and hire their mining facilities as an individual. Many other miners have formed pools over the years, and most of them offer to enter these pools.

The miners are encrypting the blocks, which takes a lot of computational resources and ensures that they can't be quickly repeated. Validating procedures may be done in a variety of ways, depending on the miner. To speed up the verification method, some miners can use various software or even create their own in-house software. It doesn't matter the tools they use, however, since all of their work would be tested. The mechanism begins when a miner collects transactions that have been transmitted on the network, checks them, and finally seals the collections of changes and activities into a new block.

For each sealed block applied to the network, a miner is rewarded with Bitcoin. Every 10 minutes, a new block is formed. As a result, each day, 144 blocks are formed. As previously stated, miners that successfully connect a new block to a blockchain are rewarded with a Bitcoin degree.

The reward for each new block creation used to be 50 Bitcoins from 2008 until 2012. The reward for a new block gets halved every four years; therefore, from 2012 until 2016, the award for each new block used to be 25 Bitcoins.

Currently, from 2016 until 2020, the award to a miner for a new block that is added to a blockchain is 12.5 Bitcoins; however, from 2020, it will be only 6.25 Bitcoins until 2024. This process will be continued until 2140 until the last Bitcoin will be created.

Block Creation

1. Begin working on a new block. And if the miners are halfway through validating a block, they would finally abandon it and focus on beginning a new one.

2. Choose a fresh transaction to work on. This is the point at which the miners would choose from hundreds of

operations transmitted across the network.

3. Check the transaction's status. If the miners discover that the payment they choose previously is not that important, they will return to number one by beginning a new block. If the requirement is high enough, the miners can proceed to the next level.

4. Verify the transaction's validity. This is a procedure that any minor must go through; there is no way for a miner to skip this stage. If the transaction is discovered to be faked or invalid, the miners must stop the operation, return to step one, begin a fresh block, and obtain another, theoretically legitimate transaction.

5. Allow the transaction to proceed. If the prior transaction was shown to be legal, it must be approved.

6. Complete the deal. If the transaction is already found to be legitimate and acknowledged, it is now time to seal it.

7. Add the activity to the block's transaction tree. This procedure can only be carried out after all the preceding procedures have been tested.

8. Examine the scale of the purchases. To seal the block, the miners must verify that there are sufficient transactions in the transaction tree. If there aren't enough transactions on the block yet, the miner won't be able to cement it until there are. As a result, the miners must return to step 2 and pick a new transaction over and over until there are enough transactions to seal the block.

9. Make sure there are no interruptions. This is the method of a miner ensuring that no other miners have locked the block with the same transactions within it in the meantime.

10. Close the block. The miners would seal the block until there are sufficient transactions for it to be sealed.

11. The block should be broadcast. The miners must broadcast the newly sealed block; but, if the miners' block sealing mechanism is broken, they can have to start a new block from the beginning.

12. Begin the latest section. This is the next move in the plan, but as you can see, we've returned to step one. As previously said, miners can be disturbed when sealing the block, and if another block of the same transaction inside a block has already been sealed by another miner, the block will not be allowed. As a result, you must begin a new block.

If you tell your friend, who has never heard of Blockchain and thinks that he or she is not affected, try to explain that everyone is affected by the Blockchain. Although Blockchain will not take over the world from one day to another, and it might require a decade or two. However, everyone is affected.

Blockchain is also known as the future of money; even though streaming money sounds weird to some, it not only will happen—but already began nearly a decade ago—and will not stop. Data protection using Blockchain will be very secured and always will provide the truth.

Because this high technology enables us to become our own bankers, we might not require having banks anymore in the future; still, because we have to look out for what we have, certain IT skills will help us to be safer from cybercriminals. Once you understand how easy it is to keep your valuables safe online, you also will realize that it is even easier than opening a bank account.

Therefore, the changes for the young and the next generation will speed up the process of learning about the crypto world. Of course, some people may have to learn the hard way, as many people have been hacked, and only after, begin to invest in learning and implementing security. Still, the time of Blockchain has begun, and it will change the world.

Average people with no technical background wouldn't believe it and probably say that Blockchain itself isn't capable of anything. However, software developers, security experts, large financial institutions, FinTech start-ups, and Banks already have paid a keen interest, as well as have begun to invest and create their protocols. Intel, Microsoft, Cisco Systems, Dell, and much more large, high-end technology firms are already all over the Blockchain and its little intricacies. Therefore, the days are counting to reach the big bang of transformation, the technology of the future, or I should say, the next Internet.

Chapter 5: Storing and Securing Your Bitcoin

Now you know what Bitcoin is and how to obtain them. There is only one more thing you need to know before you can begin using Bitcoin: storage and security. This is one of the more daunting aspects of using Bitcoin because if you make a mistake, you could lose your coins permanently. It requires some technical skill, though nothing too complex. This i'n't a section you can skip. If you do, you may as well be juggling your key-ring over a sewer grate or leaving your wallet behind in a taxi-cab.

First, let me explain some terminology. When the media discusses Bitcoin, they often say that the coins are kept in wallets, which is true but misleading. The coins are actually in their deposit boxes (their public addresses), and a wallet is simply a service that collects all of a user's deposit boxes into one place. Think of a wallet as your own little bank: you have your own row of deposit boxes and all the private keys to those boxes as well. When you need to send Bitcoin from any of your public addresses, the wallet has your private key right there for you.

This wallet can be stored in many different places. There are five main ways to keep a wallet.

#1 - Bitcoin-Qt: The Real Deal

The first option is the original option. This is the computer program (called a client) that the core of developers working on Bitcoin release every so often, with updates to make the system better.

This client downloads the entire blockchain onto your computer. Since this is the record of every Bitcoin transaction ever made, there is a lot of data to store. As of June 2013, the blockchain was about 8 GBs in size.

This standalone program has its advantages.

- When you are running the program, you are a node in the network, so you are helping the blockchain stay healthy by verifying transactions.
- You are not trusting a third party with your private keys; they are stored locally on your hard drive.
- The code is the most reviewed and most secure.

There are some disadvantages as well.

- Downloading the entire blockchain takes a very long time (hours or even days depending on your internet connection) and significant hard drive space.

- It requires time to sync with the network if you haven't run the program in a while.

- If you encrypt your wallet, then forget your passphrase; your coins cannot be retrieved.

- You are connected to the internet, increasing the chance that someone could steal your private keys.

- You can only access your coins from the computer that has the client.

While Bitcoin-Qt is a solid choice to use as your wallet, I would not recommend it for the first-time Bitcoin user. There are better choices.

#2 - The Modified Clients

There are some clients that are also standalone programs but have some different features from the main Bitcoin-Qt client. Here are a few of the more popular modified clients.

Multibit

This is considered a 'lightweight' client since it doesn't require downloading the entire blockchain and uses fewer system resources. Setting up and syncing the client is much easier and faster than using Bitcoin-Qt. For first-time users who want a standalone program as their wallet, I recommend Multibit.

Electrum

This client doesn't download any of the blockchains at all; it connects to a remote server. As such, it is very fast. It also allows users to create a 'secret seed' when they first set up the wallet. If your computer ever crashed, you could recover your coins using this system, unlike with the other clients I mention.

Armory

This client is very secure and very feature-rich. There are many neat options for users, such as creating a "cold-storage" wallet for extra security. However, this client has more features than a new user will ever need.

#3 - Accessible Anywhere: Online Wallets

You don't need to have a standalone program on your computer to use Bitcoin; you can use an online wallet. This is exactly what it sounds like: a website that offers to hold your Bitcoins in an easily accessible online wallet. This has its advantages.

- No syncing necessary; your Bitcoin is instantly available.
- It can be accessed in more places than just your computer; all you need is an internet browser.
- You can use browser plugins to make using Bitcoin online very simple.
- Your coins aren't stored on your hard drive, so if your computer crashes, your coins will still be safe online.

However, there are some significant drawbacks to using an online wallet.

- You trust a third party with your money. While several online wallets have an excellent reputation, it is still a significant risk to let another party hold your private keys.

- As I'll explain soon, if you are connected to the internet, you are already vulnerable to malicious attackers who could try to steal your coins. Using an online wallet can make that attack even easier.

- The online wallet services themselves can be—and have been—attacked. Several have been shut down because of these attacks.

So, should you use an online wallet? I do, for small amounts. It's a simple way to keep a small number of coins available if I'm going out of town and want to make sure I can access some coins easily. But I would never recommend using an online wallet for large amounts of coins.

Which wallet to use? Mt. Gox and Coinbase have wallets built into their services, and both are fine to use, but my recommendation is Blockchain. This is the most widely used online wallet, and for a good reason, it is simple but has an excellent reputation.

#4 - Bitcoin on the Go: Mobile Wallets

You don't need a computer to use Bitcoin at all—most smartphones are capable of using a wallet app. They aren't able to download much of the blockchain at all and aren't particularly secure either.

Android has many different wallets available. Check the reviews first to make sure they are legitimate. I use an app simply titled "Bitcoin Wallet." The iPhone is a little bit trickier—they, unfortunately, don't allow their apps to use Bitcoin. However, you can get a limited function wallet for download through their iTunes store.

Should you use a mobile wallet? I would definitely use one, but with the same warning as the online wallet: only in small amounts. It's neat to carry Bitcoin with you wherever you go, and if you ever do happen upon a business that advertises they accept Bitcoin, consider buying something small as a show of support!

#5 - Paper Wallet

Not only do you not need computers to use Bitcoin, but you also don't need smartphones either. In fact, you can keep Bitcoin on nothing but paper.

First of all, why would you even want to keep your coins on paper? Well, that's simple—paper wallets are, by far, the safest way to store your Bitcoin. If you have large amounts of coins, or you don't want to spend the coins but just save them, then you should consider using a paper wallet.

It doesn't seem to make sense that Bitcoin, a digital currency, would be able to be stored on paper. But remember, the beauty of Bitcoin is in public-key cryptography and the public ledger (or blockchain). To create a paper wallet, all you need to do is create a new public address and private key, put some Bitcoin in the public address, then print off the private key and store it somewhere safe. To use your Bitcoin later, you can input the private key. Often paper wallet generators create a QR code so that you can simply scan the private key.

While the process is simple enough, it gets more complicated to create a paper wallet in a totally secure way. I'll walk you through creating a secure paper wallet later, but first, you need to understand why proper storage is so important.

The Threats

You now know the different ways to store your coins, but what are you keeping them safe from? There are several threats to your digital money, and being aware of them will help you avoid them as much as you possibly can.

You are probably the greatest threat to your own coins. This may sound strange, but it's true; there are many horror stories online of people making mistakes and having lost their Bitcoin. There are two primary mistakes that Bitcoin users make. One is to encrypt a Bitcoin wallet, then forget the password. The second is hard drive damage or other technical error that causes the loss of the private key.

Some of the standalone Bitcoin clients allow you to encrypt your wallet so that if someone gains access to your computer, they cannot get your coins. However, people sometimes set up this encryption, then forget about it—until they want to spend their coins. Then they need the password—oops! They can't remember. And if this happens to you, you're sunk; there is no way to recover those coins. I recommend that if you think encryption is necessary, you should *write down your password* and keep it in a safe place. This is obviously true for an online wallet as well since you need a password to log in.

Since many users store their coins on a local drive, another problem is hard drive failures leading to lost coins. This is a shame since it is so easily avoidable: all you need to do is create a copy of the wallet file and store it on a USB drive or an online storage system, such as Google Drive or Dropbox. If you do have a backup (you should), I recommend encrypting that copy—just write down the password first!

Physical Theft: Roommates and "Friends"

While this is far from the most dangerous threat most Bitcoiners will face, coins can be stolen just like cash. If you have a paper wallet, or a mobile wallet, or a client on a laptop, a thief could simply walk off with your coins. If they know how to use Bitcoin, and they get access to your wallet, they could transfer your coins to another address they own.

This doesn't seem to happen all too frequently, but when I do hear about it, typically, it occurs in college dorms or other settings where people have tech-savvy acquaintances. If this concerns you, just keep your wallet encrypted and keep a close eye on it.

Active Attacks: Hacking

There are a few tech-savvy criminals out there who try to steal as much Bitcoin as they can.

They typically target exchanges or online wallets where there are lots of users, so individual users typically aren't at risk unless they have coins stored online.

Several exchanges have been hacked in the past few years, leading to various amounts of lost coins. As the Bitcoin community grows and as the infrastructure grows, it is likely that these types of attacks will become mitigated once bigger companies implement more rigorously tested safety measures. For now, the best approach is to store only small amounts in the exchanges or online wallets.

Passive Attacks: Malware

These are likely an even greater threat than active attacks to the average Bitcoin user since they target the individual computer that might hold the coins. A passive attack is accomplished with malicious software meant to compromise your computer. These can include things like keyloggers, which record all of your keystrokes and send them to the attacker. Keyloggers are commonly used to obtain passwords, and if an attacker has your passwords, they have your Bitcoin.

Alternatively, the malware might be a piece of software that searches your computer for a wallet file, and if it finds one, it sends that file (or just the private keys) along to the attacker.

This type of attack can even come from a browser; if you allow a bad script to run, it can wreak havoc, especially with online wallets.

This malware is unfortunately all too easy to contract, especially if you don't have good protection against it and are unsafe in your web browsing.

Avoiding These Risks

There are some specific measures you can take to avoid these risks. A few of them are simple, but some require technical knowledge and some time commitment. You determine how safe your coins are; if you don't have many coins to protect or you are so rich that you don't care, then you don't need to feel compelled to follow these suggestions.

1. Have a Clean Operating System

Your operating system (OS) is the type of software you use to run your computer. There are three main OS used today: Windows, Mac OS, and Linux. Malware is most happy running on Windows, so it is the least safe client to run a Bitcoin client on. A Mac isn't a whole lot better, but Linux is significantly safer to use for Bitcoin. If you plan on keeping a significant amount of coins on a computer, I would recommend installing a Linux distribution and learning how to use it. They are free and have nearly all the same features that their expensive counterparts have, besides being safer.

In fact, I would recommend getting an older laptop, wiping the hard drive completely, and installing Linux. Finding an old laptop online, through eBay or Craigslist, is usually simple and cheap. This gives you the most security since you are certain the OS is clean and cannot have malware. If you are looking for a good distribution of Linux (there are many kinds of

Linux to install), I recommend either Ubuntu or Mint.

2. Recognize the Internet is Dangerous

The internet is an accident waiting to happen in terms of Bitcoin safety. Your computer—and coins—have a direct connection with anyone else in the world. You have a few options to mitigate this risk. You can operate offline altogether by using a paper wallet or offline service (the Armory client allows for this).

This is the best option for large amounts of Bitcoin, and it is generally true that the more you are able to do offline, the better. Storing Bitcoin offline is called 'cold storage.'

Or you can carefully work on a computer connected to the internet. Using Linux, you will be somewhat safer since it isn't as easy for an attacker to directly access you or contract malware. If you are using Windows, you need to ensure you are up to date on your protective software. I recommend using Microsoft Security Essentials, a free program that gives excellent protection. Also, make sure to regularly update your software and run the appropriate scans to make sure you are clean. Just remember that even if your scans show you are clean, it is possible to have malware on a Windows system.

Whenever you are browsing the internet, be careful where you go and what you click on. The same is true for downloading files and torrents. Malicious software is frequently spread through falsely labelled downloads.

3. Use 2-Factor Authentication

Online exchanges and wallets nearly all offer a service called 2-factor authentication. This means that when you try to log into your account, or when you try to send Bitcoin, it requires that an outside source verify the requests are genuine and not from a malicious source. Typically, this happens by sending you a text on your smartphone or by requiring you to input an authentication code generated by a program elsewhere.

You should always enable 2-factor authentication. I use the Google Authenticator app on my phone, which I prefer, but there are plenty of other systems like this.

4. Use Paper Wallets

I've mentioned paper wallets multiple times, and that's because they are the most secure and simplest way to store your coins. To generate a truly secure paper wallet, you need to make sure that your private keys are never on an OS that isn't clean and that they never see the internet. To do that, you need to follow these steps.

1. Find a paper wallet generator that is trustworthy. I would suggest using Bitaddress to create your wallet.

2. You can print off the paper wallet from Bitaddress above, but this is not truly secure since the private keys are created by a third party *while connected to the internet*. You need to use their tools while

offline. To do this, save the Bitaddress page (as a .htm file).

3. Put the file on a USB drive.
4. Open the file on a clean OS that is *not* connected to the internet—and preferably never has been.
5. Generate a new Bitcoin address using the Bitaddress service.
6. Print off the paper wallet.
7. Delete the file and make sure that there is no electronic record of the private key remaining

On the computer or USB drive:

1. Ensure the printed paper wallet remains secure from theft, fire, flood, bugs, or other damage. If you lose your paper wallet or is it not readable, you cannot retrieve your Bitcoin! Remember, to use Bitcoin, you must have a private key that corresponds to your public address. A

paper wallet—properly created—ensures that the private key only resides on a piece of paper, and no one else can use the coins in that particular public address. That's why if you lose your paper wallet, you lose your private key, and you lose the ability to access your coins too.

2. Send coins to the public address of your paper wallet. You're done!

Now, if you want to use those coins, you import your private keys into whatever wallet you are using. Bitaddress, and most paper wallet generators, generate a QR code that allows for quick recovery of your private key when you need it by scanning the code with a smartphone or webcam.

A quick note on paper wallets: If you do choose to 'withdrawal' from the wallet, make sure you take out all the coins from that wallet at once. A paper wallet that has been used once means it is no longer a paper wallet; you will need to create a new one to be completely secure again.

Chapter 4: Cryptography

Cryptography is a process defined by data being converted into a certain form so that it is only available to those for whom it was originally intended. However, converted data is inaccessible to an unauthorized end user.

Encryption

What the process of encryption does is simple. It transforms a particular data into a form that is unreadable. The encrypted data has another common name: Ciphertext.

Decryption

The process of decryption is responsible for converting the unreadable data back into its original form so that it can become readable again. For example, a simple decrypted text, after decryption, would become plain text.

Once data has been encrypted and has been sent to the destination of the recipient, there are different ways that can be used for data decryption. There are two prevalent techniques to encrypt and decrypt data, one is using

Symmetric keys, and the other is using Asymmetric Keys.

Symmetric Key

Using symmetric keys is easy. When encrypting, as well as decrypting, we only use the same keys. An example here would be a door. When you go out to the store, you lock your door using your key, and once you return from the store, you would use the same key to unlock your door, right? Well, maybe I am wrong; however, typically, the same key is used for those purposes.

The symmetric key algorithm is very fast, in fact, a thousand times faster than using asymmetric keys. When we were talking about symmetric keys, the same keys are also called shared secrets. As you can see, the problem here is that both the sender as well as receiver must use the same key for both encryption and decryption too. Of course, this is not an advantage when it comes to security, and the blockchain is certainly not using Symmetric-Key algorithms. I wanted to introduce some of the basics before we dive into more depth, such as Asymmetric-Key algorithms.

Asymmetric Keys

Blockchain uses Asymmetric-Key algorithms as part of other algorithms it uses. Therefore, this topic is what you might have been waiting for.

Implementing an Asymmetric-Key algorithm requires having two different keys. One of them is called "Public," and the other is called the "Private" key. The reason for having two keys is simple. One of the keys will be responsible for encrypting information to become a ciphertext, and the other is to decrypt the information to become plain text. The private key would be generated by the originator, the one who would encrypt the information, and this private key must be kept secret at all times. However, the public key would be available to anyone; this is why it's called the public key.

The Asymmetric-Key algorithm is much slower than the Symmetric-Key algorithm; however, the security is more complex. Therefore, it is harder to be hacked. Both public and private keys are mathematically interconnected one to another, meaning that each public key has only one corresponding private key. There are few algorithms like that. However, blockchain is correctly using the one called: Elliptic Curve Digital Signature Algorithm.

This situation is a little different from how the Symmetric-Key algorithm works. Once the private key has been used to encrypt the information to become a ciphertext, it is necessary to use the public key to decrypt the information back to plain text. On the other hand, this process can be interchanged and used the opposite way too. For example, I would encrypt the information using the public key; then, I would decrypt the scrambled text back to plain text using the private key.

Digital Signature

When it comes to a legal contract, the traditional way to do business is that both parties, the buyer as well as the seller, have to sign the contract, amongst many other documents, for legalization. This traditional way of signing contracts is carried out with handwriting using a pen. However, there are other ways to authenticate certain documents, and one of the most known is using digital signatures.

Digital signatures are very similar to standard traditional handwriting signatures. However, they are much more secure. When it comes to handwriting signatures, there is a long history of them easily being faked by a pro or anyone with a little practice. Digital signatures have overcome the issues of counterfeit signatures by using some simple methods. The digital signature provides the unique recipient information; therefore, it provides authenticity.

- **Integrity**: This is for making sure that, while the message was in transit, it had no alteration or any modification.
- **Authentication**: This is to provide the authenticity of the sender.
- **Non-repudiation**: This is, so the sender cannot deny that the message was ever sent.

In case you're wondering how the digital signature is created, as well verified, let me begin by explaining it. Imagine that you want to create a document by adding a digital signature to it so that anyone would know that it belongs to you. What you can do first is to hash the data. Next, you can use a private key to encrypt your data. That's it, as the encrypted hash is your digital signature. Taking this further to prove that it is indeed your digital signature, you have to send the document to someone who can then decrypt your data. Once you send your text to your friend, you also have to carry the digital signature along with the document. Once your friend has received the document, he or she should decrypt your document by using your public key. This time the result of the hash value of the document would be HASH1.

So, if your friend applied the same hash algorithm on the received document, the result of the hash value on the received information would be HASH2.

Next, your friend should compare both hashes: HASH1, and HASH2 and if the values are the same, it would be proof that your document had no alteration in transit, the document is originated from you, and it is indeed yours. Today's digital world demands more flexible and responsive solutions than handwritten signatures. Instead of wasting time by using traditional signatures digitally, you can handle contracts in a matter of minutes.

Using digital signatures—deals can be closed in minutes—not weeks. Lots of software literally lets you create digital signatures in seconds. All you have to do is select a document on your computer, right-click, then choose using digitally, set your password on it, and send it off by e-mail.

The process is completely paperless, and the digital signature just as valid as the one made without ink. Furthermore, not only using a computer but a new way of using mobile apps, by having a mobile ID, you can sign documents, make bank transfers using your cell phone only. This also means that you can be anywhere in the world, and in seconds you can authorize bank transactions as well as signing any documents. Actually, research has shown that using digital signatures helps an average person save one whole week of free time every year. You may use this time as a vacation. However, there are other benefits too. Paper. We can save tons of paper around the globe using digital signatures.

Chapter 5: Bitcoin Security

You might think, "OK, fine, Blockchain is a high technology that will positively change the world." But, the question remains, "Is it secured?" The short answer is yes. But first, let's think about what the system has currently achieved. The reality is that anything can be hacked and compromised that is connected to the Internet or connected to a system that has the connection to the web. Many devices do not use any connection and can still be broken into once you have physical access to them. Such might be a laptop or desktop computer that can be broken into using a Linux cd and booted using that.

If you want to go further, let's take a look at banks, for example. They are getting compromised all the time; of course, they have stopped announcing these types of incidents, as they would have no customers left if they would carry on doing so. The director of the FBI was hacked by a teenager at the end of 2015, and most people think it's funny. Still, when you think about the security within the FBI, it is very well organized, yet still hackable. The FBI might not be the best example to mention, as even Kevin Mitnick hacked the FBI for three long years and listened to the agents' phone conversations while Agents were talking about Kevin.

Anytime they talked about Kevin as they found out where he stayed and they will raid his place, Kevin knew about it, so he just moved to another place. When you look at the NSA, aka The National Security Agency, you probably have heard of Edward Snowden already, who walked out with documents that are considered to be secret; that still shows that even the NSA has weaknesses. Confidential or even secrets can be leaked. All those expensive Firewalls, Intrusion Prevention Systems, or Intrusion Detection Systems are worthless if they are not upgraded correctly.

Also, you have to understand that having all that security does not mean anything if someone has a social engineering skillset and figures out the password to any of those devices. The result would be dramatic, and they always are, but most of the great financial institutions have stopped talking to news channels about being compromised by hackers as it would only damage their image, and it would become an embarrassment. Because companies keep all their data centralized, hackers only have to go after a specific organization to compromise its systems; that is why hackers know for a fact that anything can be broken into.

To hack into any system, it's only a matter of time and proper planning; however, when it comes to a system like Blockchain, it is highly unlikely. Although experts say that it is not impossible, it still would require an enormous amount of computing power. Blockchain has no firewalls or any Detection or Prevention system that would protect it. Instead, Blockchain's power comes from the fact that it is completely decentralized. What I mean by that is simple, really. Though, I will do my best to explain it in everyday English. Because Blockchain is an open-source technology, anyone can run the software.

You may choose not to ever buy Bitcoins or invest in any cryptocurrency. Nevertheless, you might become part of the Blockchain community by running software called Blockchain. The software itself is free to download and use, and you will have no obligation to anyone whatsoever, but once you decide to run it, you simply become part of the Blockchain community. Once you become such a member, your device will become part of the Blockchain, and each time a new block is created, your device will also get a copy of that transaction. As your device has now become part of the Blockchain, this is another device that should be hacked to compromise the blockchain thoroughly.

Because your device is now running Blockchain software, it's now also contributing to the existing decentralized system. There are no centralized copies, and every user is trusted in the same way as the rest of them. What I mean is that no master node exists, as every single device has the same replicated information, making it nearly impossible to hack. The Blockchain is running for almost a decade, and it has never been compromised, not once. It is fascinating, as the Blockchain has a bounty of 7 Billion dollars to anyone who can compromise the system, offered anonymously. Due to the price on Blockchain's head, it has become the primary target for many black hat hackers, as well as large criminal organizations, and Cyber gangs, for years.

Still, Blockchain has not been hacked yet; not even a slowdown of any kind has ever happened. This shows that the core functions have been structured very well, but, as I mentioned before, anything can be hacked, as it's only a matter of time. IT professionals always believe that with technology expanding rapidly, in the future, anything is possible. Quantum technology defines the way how the

Blockchain system can be hacked. Nevertheless, it would require hacking the million-plus machines currently running the Blockchain software.

Additionally, to actually hack all those devices, it would need to be implemented extremely quickly to be successful. Speculations about Satoshi himself are still in a shadow; moreover, as we don't know who he is and what he is capable of, one thing is for sure: he designed the system. Therefore, he would have access to the very first block that he created, and he would be able to manipulate the Blockchain system if he wanted to.

As time has passed, multiple Blockchain technologies now exist, and Bitcoin, itself, has grown its value; people have also begun to invest large amounts into various cryptocurrencies. Over the years, people have lost interest in who Satoshi Nakamoto really is, or he, just simply, has been forgotten; however, if he or she is alive and decides to manipulate the system, it could be possible, and I'm sure that the outcome would favor most.

Chapter 6: Market Manipulation and Price Prediction

In this part, I'll discuss market manipulation and how it affects Bitcoin's price. In terms of deliberately controlling the price of Bitcoin, I believe there was already a scenario, but it only started in 2017, when we all experienced a bull market. China News was constantly shown on all news channels and newspapers. Because of the low cost of energy in China, the majority of Bitcoin mining takes place there. Mining Bitcoins in China is the most efficient. Many Chinese miners have relocated their operations to other counties in less than a year. It began with China's announcement that cryptocurrencies would most likely be banned, accompanied by a decline in cryptocurrency values.

Following that, they stated that they were just considering banning Bitcoin, which caused prices to rise; however, a week later, they stated that they are considering banning Bitcoin, which caused prices to fall once more. Two weeks later, they announced that Bitcoin would not be banned, and the price of the cryptocurrency skyrocketed once again. For a moment, this was the role they were watching. In the end, the Chinese government did a great job since they were able to prohibit the majority of the exchanges. Initial coin offerings, or ICOs, were a positive thing in my mind since several of them were a fraud, yet they have managed to shut down the majority of Bitcoin mining farms.

As a consequence, the Chinese government has only been able to gain control over and operate a few exchanges and mining farms. What also happened was that Chinese people who were heavily involved in mining or operating online exchanges literally left the nation. They are now found all over the world, in countries such as Malta, where they pay much lower taxes, or

Canada and Iceland, where they no longer have to think about inexpensive mining energy. They will save much more money than before, possibly because there are fewer taxes to pay or because mining costs are lower because most of these countries are still cold, requiring no cooling systems.

Anyway, it's been a long time since I've learned anything about crypto from China, and it's possibly pointless, anyway. And what these manipulations have done is further decentralize the Bitcoin network. They intended to seize complete ownership over the Bitcoin network but actually decentralized it even more. As you can see, before all of these announcements, attacks, and ban ideas, China was expected to be responsible for 70 to 85% of all Bitcoin mining, but that number has now dropped to about 55–70%. The price of Bitcoin has been heavily influenced by Chinese news announcements.

For example, Bitcoin's valuation has risen from $6000 to $7800 after China revealed that it would reopen all Bitcoin exchanges only a month after they were closed. Because of the extreme market fluctuations, the numbers have surpassed everything we've ever seen in any other asset, and Bitcoin has been a traders' heaven! Many citizens have abandoned conventional trade of fiat currencies or precious metals in favor of learning about and investing in cryptocurrencies.

Risk analysts, technological analysts, time analysts, portfolio managers, hedge funds, and other financial institutions have begun not only to invest and trade in Bitcoin but also to advise their customers about where to store their money. Classic fund managers will advise you to keep your money in Bitcoin in 2017, but since we are in the midst of a bear market in 2018-2019, there are some fresh games that we will see all over the news. I tend to avoid naming faces.

However, there is an increasing number of hedge funds and investment managers who make various bets about the price of Bitcoin.

For example, they might declare that the price of Bitcoin would reach $100,000 by the end of 2021 and 500,000 by the end of 2022. So, they'd want to get a substantial portion of the populace to join? They don't tell you to go out and buy something; instead, they forecast. So, what happens is that a lot of people believe these hedge fund investors would know something, and then people start buying Bitcoins, stocks spike, creating a network impact to purchase, and prices go up for a while, maybe a few days or even a week, and then the price drops abruptly, right?

So, the game they play is simple: they persuade the rest of the planet to purchase, without saying so, which raises rates, and so they sell until the price is high enough for them. What they don't tell you in their public announcement is that they are in charge of other people's money because several people have invested in Bitcoin while the price was higher than it is now, and now they want their money back because Bitcoin is in a bear market, and maybe they found a better short-term investment, maybe they can't wait much longer, maybe they've run out of patience or money or both.

So, when they offer, they manipulate the market to get a higher price, and when they can't purchase themselves, they hire unqualified buyers to buy for them. They're inflating the price to get to the peak. People with strong contacts can be fairly persuasive when they get a 5-minute interview on a well-known news station, so keep an eye out for bold statements like that. I've been speaking from some of the finest technical traders, and they all believe that people who announce the price of Bitcoin over more than a few days really don't know what they're talking about or are trying to do anything by doing so.

Of course, they'd still reject market coercion, and they'd never tell someone to purchase in the first place; after all, all they do is forecast rates, right? There are several different types of market manipulations, but this forecast style has recently become quite common, so if you are a trader or wish to become a trader, you should be on the lookout for announcements like that, as they could contribute to a bull trap. Bull traps are named that for a reason: they are designed to catch bulls!

The Best Time to Buy Bitcoins

You must have heard people saying: “It’s too late to buy Bitcoins!” Or, “It’s too expensive already!” And the fact is that it’s true, it doesn’t seem to get any cheaper in terms of dollar price, but there is a reason why its value continuously accelerating, right? For example, when the first time I heard about Bitcoin, it was $300, and I thought to myself: How on earth, this Bitcoin can worth $300? I just couldn’t believe it.

At the time, I had no clue what Bitcoin was, and if I had to guess, I imagined that is a physical token of some sort. I didn’t do any research at the time, but the next time I heard of Bitcoin about 2 years later, when Wannarcy ransomware was all over the news, the price of Bitcoin was about $1700. In case it is the first time you hear about WannaCry, it was a cyberattack, lasted 4 days back in May 2017, targeting computers running Microsoft Windows operating systems, which eventually hit about 300,000 computers in more than 150 countries.

The computers became unusable, and files were inaccessible, while the Cyber gang or hackers asked for a ransom paid in Bitcoin for unlocking computers, so they can be usable again. Back to the Bitcoin price, I just couldn't believe that is gone up again so much! I thought $300 was already too much, but $1700 is definitely over the board. At this point, I still didn't buy any but began to study and learn as much as possible about the technology by reading books, blogs, forum posts, watching video courses, presentations and documentaries.

By the time I was confirmable to start investing, the price of Bitcoin was already $2400. On the other hand, you hear people who bought Bitcoins in the early days, like back in 2010, invested 20,000 dollars, when the price of a coin was about $0.20, and they are now Bitcoin millionaires, right? Well, I am not a Bitcoin millionaire, and being honest, those people had the nerve to do such a thing because they clearly didn't understand much about Bitcoin unless they were developers or have close connections to Bitcoin Devs.

But the fact is that Bitcoin had major bugs through years up until 2014, and the network was unstable, and once the bugs were fixed and Bitcoin adoption began to rise, there was a scalability issue, as the adoption rate was too high for the network, which only got resolved in 2017 by implementing SegWit, known as the segregated witness. Basically, if you started investing in the early days, when there was low adoption, no wallets, no merchants, various technical issues, like unstable network and major bugs, investing in Bitcoin was more like a gamble or a long-term bet.

Might you have heard about the Bitcoin pizza guy or the story of the most expensive pizza? If you are not familiar with the story, basically, a

Bitcoin programmer named Laszlo Hanyecz, in May 2010, posted a request that he would like to buy pizza and wants to pay with Bitcoins. Eventually, he managed to buy 2 pizzas for 10,000 Bitcoins, which was the first recorded Bitcoin payment that was in exchange for goods. This is a very famous story ever since, and people quote all sorts of figures that it was $15.000.000, or $85.000.000 worth of pizza, and some people also say that he was stupid to spend 10,000 Bitcoins on 2 pizzas. The reality is that the coins were nearly worthless at the time, didn't worth not even a penny, so Laszlo said that he made a really good deal at the time, and he had no clue that the price would ever go up in value. If you want to look at the transaction where Laszlo spent 10.000.

In BTC:

In Dollar value as of November 2020:

At the time, they said that those 10000 Bitcoins were worth about $41, and eventually, the pizza merchant also sold his 10,000 Bitcoins for $400, making 10x on his money. Yet, today those 10,000 Bitcoins worth $159,420,500. With these stories, I just want you to see that investing in Bitcoin never seem too late, and most people say that the best time to buy Bitcoins is yesterday, but my advice is that you should only buy Bitcoins once you feel comfortable doing so and don't let the price bother you, because, in the long term, the value will be increasing, anyway.

By the way, if you want to become a millionaire overnight, Bitcoin is not for you. Bitcoin, as an investment, will appreciate its value, but in the long term and not overnight.

The Worst Time to Buy Bitcoin

The actual answer is not exactly a date, but human behavior, which is called FOMO! FOMO stands for Fear of missing out, and before you think it's such nonsense, let me tell you that FOMO is very powerful, and it can move the market tremendously. FOMO can infect a wide range of people, including unqualified investors to experienced traders, even technical analysts, money managers, but even large hedge funds.

You see, FOMO is still underestimated by most people, even they know it exists, and they know they wouldn't get caught in it, but eventually, we all experience FOMO. My experience with FOMO is when the price of Bitcoin dropped from 17K to 11K, I quickly logged on to blockchain.info to buy Bitcoins, but most exchanges couldn't cope with the demand, so I couldn't buy, and the situation was very frustrating. I really felt like I am missing out on a low price, and I did, because 4 hours later, once I was able to login to the exchange, the price has increased to 14K, and guess what!?

I still bought Bitcoins even for that price because I was in such a hype to buy Bitcoins; I just couldn't wait any longer. And of course, the following day, the price went back to 11K again. After that event, we had a bear market for over 2 years where prices were stuck between 6 to 8K. That was the first time I experienced FOMO, and hopefully the last as well. You see, the prices were even 20K already, and many people speculate that it was illegal trading, or cartels manipulated the market, or it was pumped by whales because of the Bitcoin futures market, but what really happened on the market is FOMO.

Fear of missing out created a bull run since the price of Bitcoin reached about 7K and managed to triple its value. Not for long, of course, and that is because it was a HUGE FOMO on the crypto market. The problem is that most people in FOMO have no clue about Bitcoin, never watched a course, neither read a book about it, instead, heard in the news that Wall Street is about to enter the game. Especially after CME, and CBOE listing Bitcoin on the futures market, made everyone run to buy Bitcoins, and we are mostly talking about unqualified investors, having no investment advisors or money managers beside them. On the other hand, those who knew that the market is going through some crazy hype and Bitcoin is overpriced started selling and made a large profit. In the meanwhile, those who got involved when the price was about 15–18k realized that it is now back to 12K, started panic selling, which pulled the price even lower back to 10K, then further down to 8K, which was a reasonable price even before the FOMO hit the market. So, the problem with people when it comes to FOMO is that they all say things like:

"Ahh yeah, I wish I would have bought Bitcoins when it was 10K, but when it goes back to 9K, instead of buying more, they panic sell because they now fear that the price will go even lower."

So, my advice is that if you feel like you are experiencing FOMO, you should stay away from buying. Don't buy because of FOMO; it can and will hurt you, both emotionally and financially.

Chapter 7: Blockchain Attributes and Peer-to-Peer Network

Some inventors do get offended once a new and better idea takes over their own, especially if it's even cheaper, faster, or often free of charge, but this is part of the innovation that we have always experienced. When it comes to technology, and you invent something today, it's almost guaranteed that once it's on the market, there are a significant amount of people already trying to copy or make it better—whatever that service or software is. Therefore, innovation is inevitable. It is just as true when you look at physical storage for keeping data, such as music, video, or software. What happened over the years is this: the less space required, the greater the quality became; in fact, most data, movies, and music, are now streamed from multiple sources; therefore, the idea that money will be streamed one day should not be surprising. I still remember when I used to buy VHS and DVDs, also cassettes and CDs.

Also, remember when there were no mobile phones? Then, once they reached the market, I was able to make phone calls and send text messages pretty much from anywhere or even play the game called a snake.

After the introduction of the internet, I was always waiting to get home so I could access the network, or I had to call someone to check the weather forecast or other useful information for me when I needed it. However, less than two decades later, I can now store hundreds of movies and music albums on my cell phone, as well as capable of Skype, video calls, and access any internet page from anywhere in the world.

As you see, no one can predict what happens with technology over time. Believe me; the blockchain is where the internet was back in the middle '90s. The internet seemed a nerdy idea, and most people thought that it was all about e-mail. Like nowadays, some people believe that blockchain is all about Bitcoin. The reality is that e-mails might have been slow and people weren't interested in them; still, in a few years, most companies have moved online and, of course, become even more successful by doing so, and the main tool to use for both internal and external communication within the infrastructure is e-mail.

Let's take a look at them and understand a little bit more about them.

Peer-to-Peer Network

To keep the blockchain running, it requires a network that resides on the internet. Furthermore, within the network, there are certain exchanges for purposes of updates. These updates are required to continuously keep the distributed ledger system up to date with the latest block. If you turn your computer on and start to run blockchain protocol on it, it will become part of the blockchain network. Next, I would do the same with my computer;

then, my machine would become part of the network too.

Any device that is attached to the network and operating blockchain is automatically added to the network. This way, both of those machines

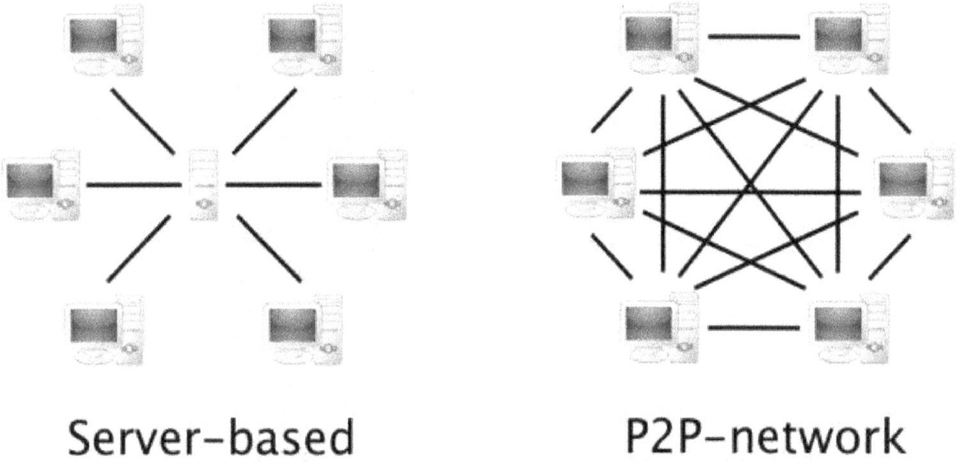

will chat with one another over the internet to hold each other up to date. This network is known as a peer-peer network, and there is no key structure or centralized machine that has a separate function from the others. Peer-to-peer networks have been used for quite some time. As a result, it contains no fresh information. This is a decentralized P2P network, not a centralized network since there are no master nodes of every sort. This is very important, as it tells you that there is no boss of any kind; so, it decreases the possibility that one or more nodes on the network might be able to manipulate the rest of the nodes. Manipulation of any kind is simply impossible, and that, in itself, is proof we can trust the system. This is not all, of course, but the network itself is solely based on a technology that's existed previously; however, this time, it has a different purpose. What you have to understand is that when it comes to a peer-to-peer network, there is no central server or central client. In traditional centralized networks, there is the primary server or central servers and multiple clients, and the way they are connected is that the servers are always dictating what the clients can have. Peer-to-peer networks, on the other hand, are completely different, as all nodes on the network serve both purposes; they are all servers as well as clients. Meaning, no one machine can have a bigger decision power than any other on the same network. Therefore, P2P networks are always working together, making decisions together, and equally distributing those to all nodes on the network.

Another problem with centralized networks is that if one node is ready to share the latest news with the rest of the network, first it would have to send the traffic to the master node or server, which then would be able to do many things. The server could manipulate the traffic before forwarding it to any other node. Managing the traffic would be easy on the server node, as once the server would receive the traffic from client A, the server would not send the same traffic back to client A (as that was the source in the first place). Instead, the server would send the traffic to the rest of the clients, but if this trade would be manipulated already, neither the remainder of the nodes nor client A would never find out about it. Another issue would also be if the server would decide to send the traffic only to a particular group of clients instead of all of them.

Again, this could reduce the power of an extensive peer-to-peer network, and in the case of the blockchain, this would not be an advantage. The worse that could happen in a centralized network is this: once the server would receive traffic for the sake of conversation, data about the latest confirmed block, imagine that the server would decide not to share this data with any other client. This would just put the blockchain out of business. Therefore, the only way that the system would operate is to use a decentralized P2P network. In case you wonder how the server would make such a decision itself, well, it would not. Even though administering a server, or a small group of servers, may be straightforward for a person; when it comes to a P2P network, a person with evil intentions, like hacking purposes, or traffic manipulations, would have a hard time to do so and the reason is straightforward. Administering a large group of machines manually that reside all over the internet is nearly impossible. This is the reason why if you want to open a company, and you want to be the boss, you would create a traditional centralized network by having a master node that you can administer anytime you want.

Again, P2P networks have no boss. Therefore, there is no one to blame, and every machine on the network shares the same responsibility.

Timing

In any system, centralized or not, there is always some delay. This is called latency. By the time one device reaches the other, it's just never the same amount of time. Technically, latency is the time defined while the data travels between its source and final destination. This is something that you may consider understanding as data propagation can take some time, especially when there are thousands of nodes on a decentralized system.

Let's look at an example for better understanding. Imagine that node A is ready to share its latest block with node B, C, and D. P2P networks are also known as dumb networks, as they have no idea what kind of data they are transferring; all they know is once there is data that needs to get transferred across the network they will do a broadcast making sure that all nodes are receiving the same data. So back to our example of four nodes and their data propagation. Imagine that node A is located in Los Angeles, US; node B is located in Sydney, Australia; node C is in Cape Town, South Africa; and node D is in London, UK.

They will all receive the same data; however, some of the nodes may get the data earlier than the other nodes. Therefore, the order of the transactions might differ on the nodes.

In summary, peer-to-peer networks are helpful for the following reasons:

- Reducing overhead by not sharing data over multiple nodes instead of keeping everything in one centralized location.
- Reducing the risk of counterfeiting and manipulating data.

Reducing third-party interference, therefore, each transaction of smart contracts has fewer fees as well as faster implementation.

Conclusion

Bitcoin is as virtual as the credit cards and banking networks that people use every day. As virtual as the money that the ECB gives to the banks and the banks give to the ECB. Money has long since ceased to be exclusively cash to be only virtual payment commitments. Bitcoin can be used to pay online and in physical stores just like any other currency if those involved in the transaction agree.

Bitcoin balances are stored in a huge network and theoretically cannot be fraudulently altered by anyone. In other words, bitcoin users have exclusive control over their funds, and bitcoins cannot vanish just because they are virtual. But bitcoin's penetration is small. And even smaller is the deployment of other cryptocurrencies.

CPSIA information can be obtained
at www.ICGtesting.com
Printed in the USA
BVHW091934300421
606221BV00013B/1942

9 781801 565028